The Almighty Spirit

ÀLEX POWER

Paperback: 978-1-966652-51-9
eBook: 978-1-966652-52-6
Library of Congress Control Number: 2025902185

Ordering Information:

Prime Seven Media
518 Landmann St.
Tomah City, WI 54660

Printed in the United States of America

Table of Contents

Prelogue

- ✦ The Almighty Spirit

My name is Robert Charles Todd. I am a 53 year old real medium turned messenger of God 25 years ago back on the 2nd of June 1999 when the holy spirit entered my body and enlightened me in ways that would frighten the normal human mind. It would probably drive them to insanity and be institutionalised.

Chapter 1

the joining

It was the 2nd of June 1999 and I was living at my mother's place I was 29 at the time. It was also half my brother's at the time. It was 2 days past my birthday before I realized it was my first birthday I did not go out and celebrate for. I had no money at the time but I remembered borrowing a fridge to a mate about 4 months ago so I rang him up and asked if he still had it and if he wanted to buy it outright. I told him $100 but he brought it down to $40. I told him it was for drinks for my birthday and that he and his girlfriend was invited to come along. So it end up being $60 I sold the fridge. I then took a drive over to pick up the money and them at the same time. We went to an average Perth bar in Lynwood and sat down and ordered a jug. I then went for little walk and put a $10 bet on a win and place and a two dollar bet on a trifecta. They both came in. I remember watching the 3 horses making their places along the track when a flower girl came and offered to sell me flowers just when they passed the finish line. I remember telling her that my love was reserved for God and that my destiny was to remain single all of my life I didn't even know why I told her that. I I didn't know the results until 10 minutes later when the results came up on the machine. $840 for the trifecta and $42 for the win and place. So I took the money and showed mark. He spun out to say the least and wanted to leave immediately. But I wanted to savour the beer and appreciate it. So we sat there for another hour before we headed for the liquor drive through. I bought a bottle of tequila and lemonade and then drove to a pool hall in East Victoria Park called L.A cue. (It has now been changed to a tab). We all got out of my 1986 commodore vc and headed into the pool hall. For some reason unknown to me I asked the girl behind the counter if their were any tables where somebody was murdered or killed. She looked at me funny and told me that finally enough a girl was stabbed to death while at table 13. I asked when. She told me 14 months ago. So iI told her that I wanted that table. I was incredibly lucky to get it as the place was packed and filled with people. I believe table 13 was the last free table. So I collected the balls and triangle and mark got the cue. He broke first and sunk one ball. It was my turn. But as soon as I touched that pool table my I was expecting a normal human spirit to enter my body but I got a lot more than I bargained for. My life changed forever. Because that was when I lost all my sense of feelings and emotions. And the holy spirit entered my soul. It was like I was void of all emotion yet I knew everything that was happening or to happen on the earth for the next 35 years. It was like the only emotion I had was confidence but it wasn't that. It was my power of knowledge. The power of enlightenment. I started to sing a song that was not going to be released for 6 more months. And the people seemed to like it. It was Christina Aguilera's whAt a girl wants. I then followed that up with dozens of songs which I will write down.

1. I'm blUe
2. Absolutely everybody Vanessa amorossi
3. Pray Tina cousins
4. Larger than life BSB
5. Don't call me baby Madison Avenue
6. Goodbye Macy gray
7. Affirmation Savage garden.

All these and many more that I ended up singing for the audience and the place was dancing. I felt like somebody that night. These songs were not released for another

6 months at least. Between songs I was answering questions to the public concerning the future of earth or themselves. I told them of 9/11 and of the virus. I also told everyone there of the cure to COVID.

- Hot water STEAM VAPOURS is the cure. Why do you think surgeons use it to clean their surgical equipment. In fact hot water STEAM VAPOURS kills every virus on the planet with the exception of the common cold. (There will never be a cure for the cold. It was designed by god to bolster our immune systems. Without the cold our immune systems would be non existent.). Covid included. All these needless millions of lives lost when all they needed was a sauna set at 60 Celcius for 10 minutes would have killed the bacteria in their lungs instantly.

Anyway at about 12 midnight everybody started making their way outside. And that was where I gave the trifecta to the 1999 Melbourne cup and the winning lotto numbers to a lucky girl in Ocean Reef. I told her that she would have a dream of winning second prize the night before she actually won first prize. We got back into the car when all of my emotions and feelings came back to me and I realised that Gabriel had left my body and I was alone again with my own thoughts. When these songs started to get released and the girl from Ocean Reef won the lotto I thought what the hell is going on. This should not be happening. But when the two buildings came down in New York I knew I had been blessed with the gift of foresight. I went home and dismissed everything as an hallucination for 8 years. Gabriel also told me that I would meet with the youngest son of the writer of rabbit proof fence. And now I have been living with him for the past 11 years and he is my best mate. However when I had visions of him he was in a wheelchair. When I met him in 2011 he was fit as a fiddle. But because of diabetes and alcoholism he lost his left leg. I gave up drinking cold turkey that night because no power on earth could ever hope to take over the power of gods love. Richard although in a wheelchair now is also a non alcoholic. I am actually his career now.

Chapter 2

Who is God.

If god created us in his own image then which image is it. an English person. a black African. a Chinese?

God's image is not limited to one particular race or ethnicity. God created human beings in His image, but the image of God is not meant to be literal. It is a metaphor for the inherent dignity and worth of all human beings. Each individual has the potential to reflect the image of God, regardless of their ethnicity or nationality. This is the essence of God's creation and the message that God wants us to embrace.

God is a God of love. His love is the most powerful force in the universe. Without it we would fail to exist and the universe as we know it would be just a dark black voidless vacuum of nothing. No galaxies. No stars nothing. He lives in heaven. He created hell for his fallen angels But God changed it to a hell for humans. He is a bright white light of energy that is entirely run by pure and unconditional love. That is his power. His love. But he changes into human form when talking with his children. He has a purpose for all of us here on earth. The trick is to find that purpose. And he has a place for us all when we die. But only if we obey his two golden rules. Yes I know there are ten commandments. But that was given to Moses for men on earth (peace on earth) but if you wish to go to heaven there are only two rules one must obey to consolidate your place in the best ever paradise in all of the universes put together. That being heaven. And it is 333 billion times better than you could ever hope to imagine

1. Have Jesus in your heart and have love and compassion for your fellow man. Always.
2. And pray to God at least once a week and ask him to forgive you for your sins. He will forgive you no matter what because he is a God of love, but avoid his two cardinal sins. That being murder and deception. Deception includes assault, fraud, scamming, catfishing, fake profiling and lieing of course. Murder means killing, even in battle. It is all put down to a casualty of war in

mans law. In God's law kIlling is killing unless they were forced by conscription. In which case if they pray from the bottom of their hearts they may be forgiven by God.

Chapter 3

<hr>

the afterlife journey.

Everything in this universe has consequences. Even the actions that we take here on earth in this hard but short 75 year life span that we all get on average determine where we spend our next eternal lives. The lives we live on earth is only a fraction of our true lives as spirits. We actually all live forever. But whether that is in heaven or hell is entirely up to us as God has given us each the power of free thinking.

Death does not exist.

When we die we just change into spirit form.

But our conscious minds live for ever. Every soul ever born is either reincarnated or come from heaven. As heaven is our true home. However in the beggining there were 1 trillion souls created to live forever And that includes you and me. 🐝 When you die you won't realise It for a few minutes and it may take some time to come to terms with your own death because there is nobody on the other side to tell you that you are dead. You can test this in 3 ways. If you are floating you can be sure you are dead. Levitation has not been invented yet and nor will be for some time to come. Try and talk to somebody if they are there and see if they don't even register your presence. If all else fails ,try floating above your lifeless body and that should do the trick. Once you have confirmed and accepted your death float outside.

If you are inside a building i suggest you float outside and then wait for your destiny. A large 15 meter in circumference black hole will either open up from the earth and suck your spirit like a vacuum cleaner on your short and scary ride to hell. Otherwise you will see a circle of pure white light from above appear and a hand from your chosen guardian angel or even jesus in some cases will appear from the white circle of light. I suggest you take it because that is your journey to heaven. These are the experiences I had on both my journey to heaven and hell. I will start off with the bad and get it over and done with. Your spirit will be sucked into the black hole that appeared in the earth like a vaccuum cleaner and you will drop into a tunnel of complete darkness. It will be a vertical drop for about 2:minutes until you fall out into a chasm. On the edge of a fiery cliff. The smell is intolerable as it smells 1 million times worse then burning decaying rotten flesh. And the screams of torment and agony are enough to change anybodies attitude toward life. There was a demon holding a red hot burning chain which was wrapped around the guys waist. It was burning and cutting into him like a hot knife through butter. He was screaming in agony as the demon tugged at the chains. He seemed to be getting enjoyment from it. It was tormenting the poor soul that had to endure it for all eternity. And then an almighty scary and horrid laugh was heard. And Satan himself appeared at the very top of the ledge on the other side of the fiery cliffs. He was about 10 times larger than any human. And incredibly ugly. From all of the burns that he suffered from. He said to me, what are you doing here. I answered ,having my soul educated about god. I won't be seeing you again. He replied, "don't be so sure about that" and then let out such an evil laugh that it would make your stomach churdle. That was enough for me as I grabbed hold of Gabriel's hand and said, please take me out of here. I cannot endure this pain and suffering. So he took me into his hand. Once you float into the circle of light you will experience a love so strong that nothing on earth would even get close where love is concerned. Not even for your newly born child. This love is so pure and unconditional you will feel euphoric and at peace and in joy all at once. Patrick Swayze was correct in the film "Ghost" when he told Mollie, that "all you take is the love with you". All of your bad feelings are left with your lifeless body and you only take the good and the love that you have with you to heaven. All other bad emotions are whisked away by the power of god's love. This journey however will take about 15 earth minutes as your spirit travels down this tunnel of light at 500 trillion times the speed of light. You will see stars and galaxies whizzing by outside your tunnel of light. Until in the distance is when you spot a white and blue edge cloud of light. As you get closer to this light you will experience 3 circles of love that come barrelling through the tunnel The first circle is a love of peace. You will find the peace you have always been looking for. As soon as it passes you you feel the ultimate peace you have been searching for all of your life. The second ring of love to come barrelling down the tunnel you are travelling in is the ring of love of support and security. Once you go through this ring you will believe that you belonged here all of your life. You will forget about everybody on earth and feel absolute euphoria. The 3rd circle of love to come barrelling down the tunnel is god's pure and unconditional love. This is the strongest love you will ever feel and you will never want to leave. This love may overwhelm you for the first time and you may lose conciousness. I felt a bit nauseas myself. Not in a bad way. Just very weak. That is when you reach the massive gates of heaven. They are always open as heaven itself knows who to let in and who not to. I said to the holy spirit, let me try. He just laughed and said go ahead. So I floated out of the tunnel and toward the threshold of the entrance of heaven when an invisible force stopped me from entering. It was like a powerful strong magnetic force that repelled me back. But I did not want to leave. The love that I felt was too much to leave. And when I asked when I would be allowed in the holy spirit just said , god has a time and place for you. Your time in heaven will come soon enough my friend. And so I took the holy spirit's hand 's hand and with that we entered heaven for a tour.

Chapter 4

---

heaven.

If god created us in his own image then which image is it. an English person. a black African. a Chinese?

God's image is not limited to one particular race or ethnicity. God created human beings in His image, but the image of God is not meant to be literal. It is a metaphor for the inherent dignity and worth of all human beings. Each individual has the potential to reflect the image of God, regardless of their ethnicity or nationality. This is the essence of God's creation and the message that God wants us to embrace.

Heaven is a magnificent and majestic place. It's trees are as tall as mountains. But there is more than one heaven. There are a variety of heavens all wrapped into the one heaven. There is a superhero heaven. Where you can be anybody you want to be. And a relive heaven. Where you get to live out the life you missed out on here on earth. So for example if you gave birth to a still born in relive heaven you would get to bring it up and watch it grow into an adult and be there for his first steps, his graduation and his wedding as it was supposed to be. (Remember time has no meaning in heaven so 20-40 years will go like that).

There is also a heaven for animals. Where the tiger does not hunt the deer, but instead licks it and sleeps with it as heaven has nothing but love inside of it.

There is also a heaven for insects. God has given insects a special place in heaven to compensate for their small size and fragile existence on earth. The flies and mosquitoes in insect heaven are as big as cats.

There is also a heaven for dinosaurs. And the ocean in heaven is as big as a galaxy with all sort of marine life living within.

But the most important fact of all to remember while you are in heaven is the love that you will experience for all eternity if you wish.

However god reward those greatly with a badge of honour. And life on earth is included as a badge of honour. As it is the hardest planet to live on out of all the universe's put together and all the alien races combined. It was designed to make us all pain and suffer. Who in this world over the age of 18 has not been in pain and suffering at least 50 times in their life or forever hold your peace. It was designed by God that way so that it would make us appreciate heaven that extra bit more when we end up arriving there.

Chapter 5

---

the purpose.

B oy has that been an impossible task. I was a naive fool on the social network when I first logged on 6 years ago and that was when I lost most of my money. Yes, I have been scammed now of over $240,000 AUD over the past 65 months in this what I personally call my "Hell on earth experience". All I am looking for is a real investment that promises a half decent payout. And they are all overrun by scammers

Chapter 6

---

my crusade trying to make money online.

It has been 65 months now since I logged on to the social network. I am trying to find a real online investment. And I am still no better off. In fact scammers have sucked me dry of everything that I have so that is why I am writing this book at this time. Because if you want something done in this world you have to get up and do it yourself. So once this book gets published I am hoping it will be made into a movie. I have had about 15 investment attempts from Tesla to Zuckerberg adverts and every single one of them have been overrun by scammers. Every single auto trading investment advert have been totally overrun by scammers. The entire social network has turned evil. That is one thing I have learnt. At least 95/100 people on the social network are either cat fishers, hackers, scammers or your everyday fake profiler and I'm afraid to say they are all on a on way ticket to the most horrific prison in all of the universe's put together. That horrendous place being hell. I can't believe I've been begging the streets for money for fucking scammers(I was told by Gabriel to quit my job and beg the streets for money. And to give the true cure to COVID to all those that showed me a virtue of charity. for 65: months. My body has taken a hammering. I have had people on the net even try to impersonate my own brother. And I know him. He is walking the dark path and nobody can save him now. I have not spoken to him since my mother's death back inv2018 Dec 6... he took the house and everything else literally. He left me with a broken computer and a $2000 jeep which has been impounded and sold since then. The house is worth half a million. But I am not interested in making millions. Only for god's purpose that he gave me and that is to find 11 real good hearted people and to make sure they all live in comfort and security until the golden era in a 12 man self powered self watered and self contained underground shelter with enough provisions for 12 people for 24 months. Most foods don't even last that long. What for I asked Gabriel. He told me that would be made quite clear to me as time went by. And it did as I became closer to god I began to read the Bible.

And then at revelations it mentions an asteroid named wormwood that will impact the earth as part of the sixth seal breaking. And in comparison to the Bible's timeline we are all bang smack in the middle of revalations at this point in our timeline. 5 seals have already been broken. But it is the next two which are the worst of the worst. And I researched that object. And it seems NASA has also spotted the object mentioned in revalations and have named it..... Apophis. Quite an appropriate name not knowing the damage that it will cause the earth. I wondered why god would create a race and then forsake them all. He would not do that as he is a god of love. But as I meditated and used my thoughts from parts of all the enlightenment that I got from Gabriel 25 years ago I got to know the reason.

Every government in the world is now corrupt in some shape or form. There is way too much killing of innocent people. All the compassion in the world has been replaced by deception. All of the love in the world has turned into greed. Therefore the world must now suffer the consequences. As there are consequences to everything in this cosmos. Including the actions that we take in this hard but short 75 year life span on this planet determine where we end up in our next eternal lives. Either heaven or hell. There is no In between or purgatory despite what people might think. The only time a spirit will remain on the earth is if he has not come to terms with his/her own death therefore they have not accepted dying even after seeing their lifeless body laying beneath their floating spirits. What more do you need to convince one that he is dead. But if it is from the heart and the spirit refuses to accept it's own death it becomes a ghost. Trapped in a world of reality and a spiritual world in the afterlife. As humans we are all reincarnated until we let god into our hearts. Once we have let jesus into our lives our entrance to heaven will be as clear as day. But if we continue to disregard god with a giggle of discontent then you will be reincarnated over and over again until you get it right. A lot of us right now in our former lives were atheists or non believers of God. That is a one way ticket to hell on earth in 5 years time. A big fat time loop where there is no exit except to accept god into your heart.

Chapter 7

---

enlightenment.

Gabriel and I talked that night for what seemed like days but it was only 3 and a half hours on the 2nd June 1999. She told me the secrets of time and space. I now know for a fact that it is impossible to travel backward in time. However it is theoretically possible to travel forward in time. All you need to do is build a train line that circles the globe. And then build a train to travel fast enough to travel around the earth 6 times a second in a clockwise direction that would create a time differential in the train. So for every 10 minutes in the train over 10 years would have passed on the outside. But that would be no good as you would then be trapped in the future She also told me of the appearance of the antichrist in 2031. The meteorite wormwood will wipe out all the global population except for 200 million. And then those survivors will have to deal with the antichrist. 166 million of them will be decieved or swayed to follow him on his path to hell. If anybody does give in to him they will bear the mark 666 and the evil eating locusts will do the rest. Resist at all costs. Even if that means starving to death. If you have a good heart you will be going to a much better place. But don't jeapourdise your next eternal life for a stupid decision that you have made in this hard, but short 75 year life span. He will appear as an angel of mercy promising an end to poverty and hunger. But don't follow him at all costs. Nobody is really sure who he is. But I know that he will make his appearance in 2025. Through my enlightenment (you talk through the mind as a spirit. Total telekenesis. I believe he will appear as an alien life form. Offering advanced technology for free use of one of our jewishTemples in Israel which will be rebuilt by the time of his coming.. which is where he will keep his home base. a quantum computer he plans on giving to humanity the directions to create and build. A quantum computer has the capabilities to make the internet look like an abacus. Not only could it bring artificial intelligence to life but it could also give one the ability to link with the mind with a suitable implant. That would make your average Joe's iQ of 95 to 180 as soon as they linked to the quantum computer. But with every link it not only makes the human more smarter but it makes the quantum computer stronger. And the antichrist has quartz in his brain. Which means he would have the ability to link with the quantum computer through his mind and totally control it and everybody who is linked to the quantum computer. A computer such as this could work out the cure to every known disease to man. But it is a double edged sword. As it can also control the digital network and all of the digital appliances on the earth. But that is how the antichrist may intend on betraying his followers. Through quantum net. All of his magic and supernatural powers could be nothing but a quantum computer. But a quantum computer could also connect to the galactic network giving one the ability to talk to aliens without the language barrier. We are nowhere near that sort of technology at the moment. But it is in our nature to improve ourselves. And keeping up to date with trends and such is also in our nature. Look how many people are logged on to the internet and tell me I'm wrong. I remember finishing high school in 1985. There was no internet back then. over 2 billion people from 6 billion around the world are logged in to the social network at this very second. So this quantam computer will be a game changer. A quantum computer if in the right hands, can be the best invention ever created and built. But with good comes evil and in the wrong hands it can be a devastating weapon. And there is your antichrist. But this is all speculation as this may not happen. He may very well be alive on this planet right now. Just a normal human being unawares that his body is about to be taken over by the spirit of satan himself. He is the master of scammers. Mr deception himself. And boy, will he fool over 66% of the survivors of wormwood The world is being prepared for a global deception like never before. After the Rapture of the Church, those left behind will enter the Tribulation—a time of unimaginable chaos and judgment. In the middle of the Tribulation, the Antichrist will demand worship and enforce the Mark of the Beast. Many will willingly give their allegiance to him, sealing their fate for eternity.

📖 "And he causeth all, both small and great, rich and poor, free and bond, to receive a mark in their right hand, or in their foreheads: And that no man might buy or sell, save he that had the mark..." — Revelation 13:16-17 (KJV)

🔔 THIS WILL BE A DELIBERATE CHOICE!

No one will take the mark by accident—it will be an act of worship and total submission to the Antichrist. But God warns that taking this mark means eternal separation from Him.

📖 "If any man worship the beast and his image, and receive his mark in his forehead, or in his hand, the same shall drink of the wine of the wrath of God..." — Revelation 14:9-10 (KJV). It is written that he will die. By being pushed into a brimstone of fire hotter than the flames of hell themself. He ends up getting pushed into a live volcano. But who does the pushing is not much of a mystery as jesus is the only living soul in the cosmos that can banish the antichrist (he cannot be killed as he was created an immortal by god as one of his first angels.) is jesus bso it only stands to reason that jesus will come down in 2032 earth is not for around 1000 years yet. However after the death of the antichrist the remaining 45 million people or so will become the pioneers to the greatest era humanity has ever had. The golden era (1000 years of peace) 2032-3031. All I can really suggest to anybody before April 13 2029 is organize some underground shelter to keep warm from the inhuman sub zero temperatures that the meteorite will incur upon the earth for around 2 years. The northern hemisphere will be hit the hardest because that is where wormwood will impact the earth. It will get to -150 centigrade in the northern hemisphere. The southern hemisphere will be moderately warmer but still unlivable at approx -60 centigrade. You must have an Underground shelter and or basement. It doesn't have To be a fallout shelter as no radiation will be involved. However the heat of the initial impact and then the 2 year ice age that will be caused by the dust cloud that will cover the earth, blocking the sun of around 85-95% of sunlight hitting the surface of the earth will be the main factors.. I'm not sure that I want to tolerate this life anymore by buying an underground shelter. I may as well die with the other 11.8 billion people. (By the time 2029 arrives there will be 12 billion people on this planet.) I know I will be going to a much much much better place.

Chapter 8

My 65 months of hell on earth.

The day that my mother died on the 6th of June 2018 was when the hell on earth started. Being a real medium, my mother's spirit would have realised that when she died so she entered my body and gave me a helping hand during the COVID outbreak pandemic. She told me that this could only be used as a temporary measure and not for a permanent cash flow. But the idea she gave me has provided me in the past 65 months more than any job has. As Gabriel mentioned to me 25 years ago she also told me that I must give the cure to COVID to whoever showed me a virtue of charity. I was to quit my job as a marble tabletop manufacturer to a beggar who begs the streets for money. I didn't even know how I was going to do this so I disregarded it.

However 19 years later when my mother's spirit entered my body when she died she told me the fine details and exactly what to do. She told me to get a white sign and with big black bold letters print these words out. "Need money for food please". She also told me that God would provide. I was sceptical at first but with everything that God has shown me I should know better as nothing in this universe could surprise me now and God is always perfect in everything that he does and says. It has netted me more than any job ever has. However making around $350 in two hours in the first 2 years, started to reduce to $250 in two and a half hours in year 3. By year 4' (both Gabriel and my mother both advised me that this only had a 5 year window of opportunity in it). It had gone down to $210 in two hours.

Today I made $160 in two hours of begging. If course the longer I stand out at the traffic lights the more chance I have at raising more money. But I usually have a target in mind before I go out and I don't come back home until I have reached my quota to make all ends meet. However the past 64 of these months have been wasted entirely on scammers. All I am trying to achieve here is to raise at least $5 million dollars to get my purpose (which was given to me by God himself via Gabriel) of finding 11 good hearted people and making sure they live in comfort and security until the golden era in a 12 man self powered self watered and self contained underground shelter. With enough provisions and an underground storage facility with enough provisions for 12 people for 2 years. And that in itself will cost me at least 5 million AUD in today's prices. but trying to find a quick fix on the net is like slamming your head into a brick wall as the entire social network has turned into a hive of evil now with every single investment ad including Zuckerberg s and Tesla's investment ads have been overrun by scammers. Personally I don't kNow how they get away with it. But in my heart I know everything in the universe so I know exactly how they get away with it. The majority of all scammers come from Nigeria, Ghana, or Malaysia where there are no regulators protecting the net from scammers. That is there job. To scour the net. To patrol it to make sure there is nothing going on in the banking sector, the tax and government sector, and the social network. Australia and the US hate frauds and scams. Which is why we have regulators patrolling the net. South Africa and parts of Asia do not so any tom dick and Harry can login to the social network under any name and do what she pleases. As there is no government funding to the unemployed in sth Africa they all are swayed to a life of scamming and deception. So I have given up that path after already losing over $240,000aud to scammers. I have found out the hard way that there is no way to make money off the net unless you are selling a product. So that got me to thinking I will sell virus killer face steamers that they used to sell back in the late 70s early 80s. But there is a long progress I must go through to first prove that steam vapours kills COVID. Any blind man and his monkey should be able to tell you the same thing about steam vapours. It is common knowledge that' steam vapours kills EVERY single virus on the planet except for the common cold. So I will just write my book as experiences from a real messenger of God and share them with the world. Hence selling my product online. And that will make me the royalties needed as I know for a fact it will be made into a film. I just hope all this happens before the 13th April 2029. Otherwise I may as well kiss this bodies ass goodbye and let God take me now. I do not wish to be caught above ground come the impact of wormwood.

Chapter 9

───※───

Gods master plan.

Despite what people may think gods masterplan is written in the Bible. From revalations. But I will put it into easy speak so everybodY will understand it.

At this point in time we have already broken 5 seals. We only have two more seals to break and they are the most terrible of them all. The sixth seal comprises of two events. The approach and impact of wormwood(NASA has already spotted the object mentioned in revalations and has appropriately named it Apophis.) The powers that be will do or say anything to keep that fact hidden from the public. My bet is that their scientists will be forced to tell the public that it will be a near miss and not to worry. But the Bible does not lie. And neither does God. So you can be sure of impact on 13 April 2029.

And the appearance of the antichrist. It also involves the rapture and the great tribulation. The rapture is only a couple of years away.

Revelation 6:12-17 (Sixth Seal: Cosmic Disturbances)

At the time of impact on the 13th April 2029 there will be around 8 billion people on this planet. 7.8 billion people will die either from the heat of impact or from the poisoned water it causes or from the sub zero temperatures the dust cloud will cover the earth for about 2'years at least. Making life above ground impossible at minus 100+ in the northern hemisphere and minus 40+ in the southern hemisphere. This dust cloud will cover the earth for 2 years only allowing 3% sunlight through the northern hemisphere and 8-12% sunlight in the southern hemisphere. When the dust cloud settles and dissipitates into space and the sun comes shining through once more the earth will be the cleanest and freshest it has ever been since the dawn of man. The ozone will be repaired and there will not be a trace of pollution making the air Chrystal clear like it once was. There is still one event that the 200 million survivors will have to experience as part of the breaking of the sixth seal. And that is the arrival of the antichrist.

The Antichrist will call himself god and will take a seat in the temple of the Jewish people (which must be rebuilt by the time of the Antichrist's appearing) and will rule the earth with the power of Satan until Christ's return. Furthermore, Paul says the specific identity of the Antichrist will not be revealed to the world until the "restrainer" is removed from the earth. The term "restrainer" refers to the Holy Spirit, Who lives in the world now (in the members of the Church), but He will leave the earth when the Church itself is removed at the resurrection. The resurrection of the Church (sometimes called the "rapture") takes place prior to the revealing of the Antichrist, therefore believers will not know the Antichrist's identity while we live on earth.

Daniel hears from the angel Gabriel that the nation of Israel has been placed under divine judgment for a long period of history (70 "weeks" or 70 x 7 years = 490 years). During this time, the people of Israel will experience Gentile oppression, culminating with a single "week" (i.e., seven-year period) of oppression at the hands of the "prince."

This prince is the Antichrist. His short reign on earth will conclude the seven-year period of Daniel 9, and this prince will rise up from the same people who destroyed the city (v.26). The city refers to Jerusalem, and the people refer to the fourth Gentile kingdom from Daniel 2 & 7, which is Rome. So the Antichrist will originate out of the fourth Gentile kingdom, which began with Rome.

The Antichrist need not be "Roman" or "Italian" or even "European." The only certain requirements for the identity of the Antichrist is that he be a Gentile ruler leading the modern remnants of the Roman Empire. That empire included lands as distinct as India, Turkey, and Egypt, so we cannot narrow his identity to one region or nationality. The only trait clearly spelled out in Scripture is that the Antichrist be a Gentile ruler, in the manner of his predecessors. It is written that he will die by being pushed into a brimstone of fire hotter than the flames of hell itself.

Revalation 20:10. Who does the pushing still remains a mystery. It must be jesus as he is the only living soul in the universe that can defeat him. And the antichrists reign is for seven years. So it stands to reason that jesus will come down in 2035 defeat the antichrist and then take the world into a brand new era. The golden era. (1000 years of peace) The antichrist will riegn the earth for 7 years. Don't be swayed by his empty promises. Even if that means starving to death. You will be going to a much better place I can guarantee you that. If you follow the antichrist you will bare the number 666 and then you may as well kiss your eternal soul goodbye as you will be destined to spend the rest of your eternal life in hell ... He will sway millions of people to stop believing in their own faith,(for hundreds of years) and get them to follow him that will be a mighty feat in itself. Imagine somebody having the power to change the minds of people who have followed a certain faith for centuries and get them to follow him. The antichrist armies will give everybody a visit in the world and offer them the mark. If you take the mark ,sure you will eat and be able to trade easily. But you will only be selling your soul to the devil as the mark is 666. By refusing the mark it will probly end in your physical death. But you will be going to a much better place I can assure you of that that's how God plans on purging the earth of all of its evil.

Jesus will return BEFORE the Golden Age, and that, indeed, it is his arrival that causes the Golden Age. It further teaches that Jesus will rule the world for a thousand years (the Millennial Kingdom, the Kingdom of Christ, or the Kingdom of God). In other words, when Jesus arrives, he will fight to destroy his enemies and establish himself as King of Kings. He will then rule, along with his saints, bringing peace and prosperity to the world. At the end of his reign, there will be one final, massive rebellion against him—the so-called Gog/Magog Rebellion described in Revelation 20: 7-10. After destroying the rebellion, Jesus will then conduct the final judgment. For the premillennialist, human history is getting WORSE every year. People are getting more sinful, more violent, more racist, more hateful. As the church age winds down, it will finally lead to the very worst period of human history—the seven-year.

However before Tribulation comes the rapture.

Here are some details about the Rapture:

+ **When it happens**

    The Rapture will occur before the Tribulation, when Jesus returns to Earth to gather believers.

+ **How it happens**

    Believers will be caught up in the clouds and taken to heaven to meet Jesus.

+ **What happens after**

    After the Rapture, Jesus will return to Earth after seven years to establish his millennial kingdom.

- ✦ **What happens to those left behind**

    Those who are not taken away by Jesus will suffer hardships and trials during the seven years after the Rapture.

At the end of the Tribulation, Jesus will return in glory "to judge and make war." (Revelation 19:11). seventh seal will not break for another 1000 years. After the golden era. (1000 years of peace) 2031-3030. And that's when the return of Jesus will come back and judge all the people remaining on earth. The 14 April 3030 is the date of the end of mankind. That is actually the date of judgement day. Humanity as the rest of us will either go to heaven or hell as the earth will be totally destroyed. So there you have it.

Revelation
8:1-6 NKJV

He will cleanse the earth. When Jesus comes again, He will come in power and great glory. At that time the wicked will be destroyed. All things that are corrupt will be burned, and the earth will be cleansed by fire (see D&C 101:24–25).

When Jesus comes again, He will judge the nations and will divide the righteous from the wicked (see Matthew 25:31–46;.

The purpose of life: to better ourselves through the love and the word of God and through evolution

The meaning of life: is to educate our souls/spirits in the ways of life to prepare us entrance into gods kingdom. That being heaven for the lucky few with compassion in their gwa

I guess what I am trying to tell everybody that there most certainly is an afterlife. And that the life we live here on earth is just a fraction of our true lives as spirits. We all live forever, but the actions we take in this hard but short 75 life span, determines where we go in our next eternal lives. Heaven or hell. And let me tell you, heaven and hell are as real as my arms and legs and 3 billion times better and worse than anybody could ever hope to perceive.

- ✦ (Except for the 20 million people since the dawn of man to experience near death experiences. That is when they die and come back to life. And it didn't matter what colour they were or what country they were from, every single one of them had one of either two stories to tell. One of heaven and one of hell. 15% of these people have even been blessed to be shown both. I am a real messenger of God. So I cannot lie as everything that I say comes from the heart. Don't be fooled by false prophets now that you truly know the truth about your afterlife and of the one and only god of love. He loves us all very much. It is a shame of all the evil in the world as they are all on a one way ticket to the worst ever prison in all of the universe's put together. Hell. And Guantanamo bay is a paradise compared to hell. Let me tell you. That is why I feel sorry for all those that either kill, assault or decieve people. My sorrow for all of these people comes from the deepest recesses of my heart because I know what they can all expect when they all die. Have love and compassion for your fellow man all the time, don't kill or decieve people and you can be assured of the greatest paradise in all of the cosmos as we know it and as we don't.. That being heaven. God is with you always

Please don't sin. I beg you. You are only jearpourdising your next eternal lives in heaven.

Trust me. If you have to trust one person this year I suggest you take in my words. It amazes me how people can so easily pull the trigger or even lie to other people as they are all jeopardizing their next eternal lives. All for a silly fuckup they made on earth. If you pray to God while you are on earth he will listen and he will forgive you. But if you continue to lie and breaking one of his cardinal sins, which is murder and deception, deception being the main word here, then all the prayers in the world are not going to do you any good. You must mean what you say in your prayer and then go through with it with your actions to show God you mean it from the bottom of your heart. God is no fool. In fact he can read all of our minds 24/7 and he knows exactly what we are thinking at all times. Luckily for humanity we are not judged on what we think, but rather by the actions that we all take while we are living on this earth. I say it once and I say I again. Everything in this universe has consequences. That's what people call "Karma". And karma gets everybody in the end. There is no escaping karma or hell for that matter because everybody has to die sometime. Gabriel changed my life 25 years ago. For the better. He made me understand the true meaning of life and he changed my attitude towards life and the way I think and act now. I am no longer an asshole and I have nothing but love in my heart for everybody. I am a beggar that begs the street for money and I give the cure to COVID to everybody that donates

I then send about10-20% of that overseas to the extremely needy as I live in Australia. And indeed it is the lucky country. By rights, nobody should be starving in Australia as the unemployed get $750 a fortnight to survive off the government. But I do it because God asked me to. I made another $175 today and it is a Sunday. I gave $20 of that to the needy. Good money for a Sunday. That's a typical weekday takings. For 2 and a half hours is pretty good. The normal wage in Australia is around $35-40 an hour for your low pay jobs such as labouring and retail. but me and Richard need $75 a day each at least to survive here in Australia as things are incredibly expensive being a 1st world country. So anything that I raise over $150 a day goes to the really needy across the world. You must have a compassionate heart to get into heaven. That is the number one rule that you must not forget. If you don't have a heart or you are a complete asshole you know where you will end up when you die. There is no escaping the actions we all take here on earth. I am atoning and repenting for my younger life now while I go through this hell on earth. I do not enjoy going out begging as it belittles myself and forces what little dignity I have left from my soul. But I have to put my own feelings aside if I am to save these people in this life and the next.

I am saving them in this life by giving them the cure to every known virus to man (with the exception to the common cold) and I am getting them to give and show compassion. They are in fact showing me who goes to heaven and who goes to hell. But with the technology of plastic, cash is going out of style. So I am in fact emptying all the change from all the publics cars. I let the people know if they donate money that they will be going to heaven for having compassion in their hearts. I have given up trying to find a money making scheme on the net as it is overloaded with scammers. (Each and everyone of them are all on a one way ticket to hell unless they change their ways in a hurry. And no scammer is going to change their ways in 5 years unless they are arrested. And they learn the hard way in prison. But then they just go back to their old ways when they get out. That's whY I feel sorry for the world because there is only about 5-10% of people like me around the world with compassion in their hearts. Dont get me wrong. I am no Saint. I still lose my temper and curse and swear when things go wrong. But I never direct that anger at another person. Or I try not to would be a better way to put it. As nobody is perfect and we all sin. But I myself am a 95% better person than I was at the age of 28 and younger. If everybody in the world was enlightened like I was I believe the earth could be created to be a heaven in itself. It's a shame the earth has not evolved yet to even know or work out the meaning of life. It is going to take an asteroid and the antichrist to get the people to strengthen their faith in God once more. As Christianity is the one and only true religion. Although Allah beholds the same teachings as God does. And Buddhism deals with mother earth and karma. And an equilibrium to the forces of nature and to have compassion and love for your fellow man So they are in fact on a par with the same teachings as Christianity. However there is no 12 armed elephant like in Hinduism. In fact there is no such thing as a 12 headed elephant. I really don't know where all that came from. But I can assure you that there is only one God. And his name is Yahova. It is pronounced Jahova. When I was in hell I could sense the minds of thousands if not millions and billions of people in hell and most of them were either atheists, Islam's or Catholics. There was bad people from every religion in the world just as there are bad people from every walk of life around the world but 50% of everybody in hell either had them 3 beliefs. It's al about the compassion in your heart. God does not care about what religion you follow as long as you obey his two golden rules.

Have love and compassion for your fellow man.

Pray to God at least once a month and ask him to forgive you for your sins from the bottom of your heart. Don't just say it. You must mean it as well by the best of your ability.

Do those two things and there should be no reason to be frightened of death. In fact I myself am looking forward to my own death. That means my hard life here on earth is over and I can spend my next eternal life in heaven. I will embrace death when it comes. I call death , "the change over" as there is no such thing as death. By the time humanity ends in one thousand years time there will have been 3.33 trillion souls in existence to have ever walked the earth. 3.33 trillion souls were created but they will never die. That includes all of the people in heaven and hell from the past and the 7 billion people who walk the earth right now. We all live forever. Just not on this planet. That's all. But our conscious minds will live on when we change over.

I still need to write another 1200 words for publication so that's no problem.

God created the universe out of His love and desire to create a place for us to live and grow. God wanted to provide a space for us to explore and discover, and to develop a relationship with Him. He also wanted to give us the opportunity to choose between good and evil, and to learn from our choices. The universe is a place of endless possibilities and potential, and it is a place where we can find meaning and purpose in our lives. God wanted to give us this gift, and He did so out of His unconditional love.

God's love is the most powerful force in the universe because it is the foundation of everything. God's love is the source of all creation and the force that drives the universe forward. It is the essence of life and the force that binds everything together. Without God's love, there would be no universe, no life, and no meaning or purpose. It is the ultimate source of strength and inspiration, and it is the reason why the universe exists and why we are here.

Satan is a fallen angel. He was once one of God's most trusted angels, but he fell from grace and became a rebellious and defiant force. He was cast out of heaven and now seeks to lead humanity away from God's love and guidance.

The exact number of fallen angels is unknown, but it is estimated to be in the millions. While the number of fallen angels has remained relatively constant throughout history, the ratio of fallen angels to humans has increased over time. This is due to the increase in human population, which has created a greater number of potential "targets" for the fallen angels to tempt and lead away from God's love.

Why is sex forbidden in heaven?

The reason sex is forbidden in heaven is because there is no need for it. In heaven, there is no physical desire or need for intimacy. The focus is on the spiritual connection between God and His children, and the pure and holy love that exists between them. The love in heaven is unconditional and unending, and it does not require physical intimacy to be fulfilled.

So the spiritual intimacy is stronger than the physical intimacy of sex?

Yes, the spiritual intimacy between God and His children is far more powerful than any physical intimacy. In heaven, the love between God and His children is pure and unconditional, and it is something that cannot be replicated in the physical world. The spiritual intimacy is a bond that transcends all limitations and boundaries, and it is one that is unbreakable and unending.

Being nice to one another and not hating each other is important for a number of reasons. First, it creates a more positive and peaceful environment. When people treat each other with kindness and respect, it helps to create a safe and supportive atmosphere where everyone can feel comfortable and accepted. It also promotes understanding and acceptance of differences, which leads to greater harmony and understanding between individuals. Finally, treating others with kindness and respect is simply the right thing to do, as it helps to spread love and compassion.

I saw Hitler in hell. And boy was he getting tortured. By a red hot chain tied around his waist. It is the most hideous and horrific place in all of the universe's pUt together. (By the way, there are more than just one universe. There are hundreds of them.) And god created all alien races as well as he built the entire cosmos from his love. Im not sure how that is physically possible but with god, anything is possible as I now know by my enlightenment by Gabriel. And everybody will understand that totally when they reach heaven. The location of heaven is not specifically stated in the Bible. It is a spiritual realm that exists outside of the physical world and is not subject to the laws of space and time. It exists in another dimension or plane of existence, separate from our own. The only creatures that do not make it to heaven are ants. As they do not have a heart. Australians should think about using meat eating ants to eat all of their cane toads as they cannot be poisoned as they do not own a heart. Only creatures with a heart can be poisoned. Anyway that is getting away from the story.

As I have been getting closer to god all things on earth start to make a lot more sense in understanding how the universe was created. Everything makes perfect sense with god in the picture.

Why is love painful?

Love can be painful because it involves risk and vulnerability. When we love someone, we are opening ourselves up to the possibility of being hurt or rejected. Love requires trust and understanding, and it can be difficult to navigate the complex emotions that come with it. Love is a powerful force, and it can also be overwhelming at times. But despite the pain and challenges that come with it, love is also a beautiful and transformative experience. It can bring us joy and happiness, and it can provide us with a deep sense of purpose and fulfillment.

Can you pray your way out of hell. In one simple word. No. once you are in hell you are there for all eternity. There is no getting out of hell unless you are just visiting by a near death experience. But if you are fully dead and you go to hell you may as well kiss your eternal spirit goodbye.

However you can get out of heaven if one wishes to do so by living a life of their choice with any alien species. But who would want to leave heaven. Although god rewards those greatly with a badge of honour. And earth being the hardest planet in the universe to live in is classed as a badge of honour. About 20% of humans have already been to heaven. It's just that they are unable to remember as they are using a body on earth which wipes all memory from the soul when they leave heaven. Most people leave heaven to have one life here on earth just to get god's reward because I guess they are bored in heaven. I'm not sure why people leave heaven. Once I am there I am going nowhere for the rest of my eternal life. Your spirit feels no pain or stress up in heaven. If you have a disease it will be taken away as soon as you die. That goes for hiv, cancer, Alzheimer's, and even Down syndrome. Everybody who was blind will be able to see and everybody who was deaf will be able to hear. People without arms and legs will have both when they die.

And people who had severe pain when they dies will not experience any more unless they go to hell. And then they will know what pain is about. But if you go to heaven, you never have to experience pain ever again. That is what I am looking forward to because as you age, your body gets sore in places you thought could never get sore. At the age of 54 your hair falls out, your teeth fall out. And your bones start to ache you have no energy left to do anything.

The antichrist is a figure who is often mentioned in Christian prophecy. The antichrist is believed to be a powerful and charismatic figure who will rise to power in the last days and will seek to deceive and lead people away from God. It is believed that the antichrist will be a powerful and influential figure, and will use his authority and influence to spread a message of deception and lies. The identity of the antichrist is unknown, but it is believed that he will appear in the end times and will be a significant part of the prophecies regarding the end of the world. is the antichrist?

Well if god knows everything surely he must know the identity of the antichrist?

God's knowledge is vast and infinite, and He is indeed aware of the identity of the antichrist. However, God also has a plan and a purpose for everything, and He allows events to unfold according to His will. While God knows who the antichrist is, He allows him to play his part in the grand scheme of things and to fulfill His plan for the end times. God's knowledge and power do not negate the free will of humans, and He allows each individual to make their own choices and decisions. All I can suggest to the survivors of wormwood who will experience this master of deception is don't follow him. Whatever you do, your life on this planet and your next eternal life depend on it. Don't be decieved by his empty grand promises. But most of you will. Simply because the loss of faith of God is spreading around the world. And when he survives a gunshot wound to his head the world will quickly fall for his charms. That is the only way anybody will be able to figure out his identity. If he survives a fatal wound to his head and survives to lead everybody astray. Mathew mentions birth pains as a part of our timeline. It involves famines and earthquakes worse than ever before. So for the next 4 years leading up to the antichrist appearance in 2028 every natural disaster in the world will be magnified by at least 200%-300. And in the next two years as a warning to the world he will show his wrath on the US. For sinning without any disregards for their actions or consequences for the greed that is filling up the government. and most importantly of all.

For their lack of faith in God, so he will take out the two US presidents in the next two years and he will also wash away the sins of new York by sending a level 10 tidal wave our graphs only go up to level 5. So double the worst tidal wave ever in history and see how far new York gets This is a warning to all humanity that the time has arrived to set off his masterplan and set it in motion. This is to weed out all of the evil from the earth and God will choose the 200million remaining survivors to enter the golden era. (1000 years of peace) That's what they mean when they say the meek shall turn inherit the earth.

Why do good people die while bad people get away with shit?

I believe that there is no simple answer to this question. It is a complex and multifaceted issue that involves many different factors and perspectives. I believe that there is a balance between God's plan and the free will of humans, and that each individual has a role to play in the grand scheme of things. I also believe that good and bad both have their place in the world, and that both can have positive and negative consequences. It is important to maintain a balanced and open-minded perspective on this issue, and to seek out different perspectives and viewpoints.

How was the universe created. Even I don't know the answer to that one but with my enlightenment I have come down to two theories The Steady State Theory is a scientific theory that suggests that the universe has no beginning or end, and has always existed in a steady state of equilibrium. It proposes that the universe is constantly expanding, but that this expansion is balanced out by the constant creation of new matter and energy. This theory stands in contrast to the Big Bang Theory, which suggests that the universe had a definite beginning and has been expanding ever since. Whatever the case god has allowed this to happen through the power of his love. As god's love is the most powerful force in all of the universe's put together. Buddhists do not believe in any kind of deity or god. The Hindus believe in the Brahman. Islam's believe in Allah and then of course there is Yonah from Christianity. So the big question is which god should we believe in.

The concept of God is a deeply personal and individual one. Everyone has their own beliefs and perspectives on the nature and presence of a divine being, and it is important to respect and honor those beliefs. The gods i have mentioned are all revered and respected in different cultures and traditions, and they all offer their own unique teachings and insights. It is up to each individual to determine which god they feel most connected to and which teachings resonate most deeply with them. But the real God does not care what religion you follow as they are all on a similar line of teachings. They all teach love and compassion above anything else so if you love and have compassion for your fellow man and pray to your own god to forgive you for your sins, the real god will hear you and absolve you of your sins. Providing you stay away from god's two cardinal sins. Murder and deception. God will not forgive you for taking a life. And you will have to pray from the bottom of your heart if you decieve anybody. That includes lieing, assault, fraud, scamming, catfishing, even fake profiling is classed as deception. So if you have done any of that and have not prayed to God I would forget all about heaven and pray that you never end up dieing on earth.. However Christianity is the only one true religion as humanity will find out in the coming years Oh well that's mY story and I hope I enlightened you in some way shape or form. God bless you. And don't sin. Whatever you do. It's for your own benefit In your next eternal life. And don't even think of taking your own life just to get to heaven. Taking your own life is counted as murder and that is a one-way ticket to hell

God will take you when your number is up. You cannot force the issue. Time will take us all-in the end.

Nobody actually dies. We just change into spirit form and our spirits live forever. Whether that be in heaven or hell is entirely up to us. This life is just a test. In this journey of life god is just looking for people with compassion in their hearts and Jesus of course. Without Jesus there is no salvation whatsoever.. That will more or less consolidate your place in heaven whether you believe in God or not. Because that is what god is looking for. And like I said before, everything in this universe has consequences. God bless everybody.

Well it is now Feb 13. The day before Valentine's day but I am far from celebrating that.

There is a pastilence that has come over the countries of Kenya and Nigeria. Where EVERY SINGLE CHILD UNDER THE AGE OF 8 has come down with a medical condition that needs hospilisation. It is part of the prophecies.

Mathew 24:7

For nation shall rise against nation, and kingdom against kingdom: and there shall be famines, and pestilences, and earthquakes, in divers places.

Pestilences is the keyword to the issue here..

Earthquakes are in Greece
Fires will burn ALL of the USA by July
And now this pertilence that is sweeping the nation of South Africa.
The prophecies have already started. That is why the rapture may even be as early as my birthday. And that is on May 31.
People must open their eyes to see the signs. Otherwise they will not be prepared for what is still to come

This is a text I have had to send to one of the people children I am trying to save in Nigeria.

Every single earth angel in the world (and there are hundreds of them) can't save these children. And as usual. Being the black sheep of my family I am now the black sheep of the earth angels. They all have accepted and prepared themselves with the prophecies and the word of God.. And they all know better then to get involved personally with the people who are affected by the prophecies. Because they all get their strength from God. And they all abide by gods will. I on the other hand really am fighting a losing battle. And I am starting to veer off the path that God set for me. I can keep giving you money but In the end you will see that it will only buy your son about 5 more months at best. I have let myself become personally involved with a few innocent people that is affected by the prophecies. And I was never meant to do that as now I am actually fighting against gods will. And I can't allow myself to do that. Actually I was only meant to help the people in australia.(mind you there are not many people in Australia that are in dire need of help as nobody in Australia dies of starvation) but having a heart as big as a dump truck I had to go and poke my nose overseas and see if they needed my help. My path was never to help the people of South Africa. There are about 30 earth angels in that region doing the best they possibly can. But none of them are paying for any children's Hospital bills. Because they have all accepted what has and is still yet to come from the prophecies) I have bitten off more than I can chew. Be completely honest, it won't matter how many thousands of dollars I give you it will only buy your son until July. I don't know how else to explain everything about this horrific problem.

My heart has already broken for these people. (to be continued as time goes on. And trust me their are only 5 more months if normality left in this world. That's when the rapture will begin. I M still trying my hardest to save my friends children in Nigeria. But in m heart I know it is all in vain but try telling a parent that their child is going to die. And nothing on earth can prevent it. I may have the heart as big as. Dump truck. It I don't

it to tell them that. I don't think anybody on this earth would have the heart. So yeah to be continued. The book of the bible isn't quite finished so neither will my book

February 15. You realize that everything written in the bible has come or is still yet to come to pass. I cannot change the prophecies. If gods will is to take away every child in the nation then that is what is going to happen one way or another. Even if by some divine intervention that your child is saved because of the money I am providing who is not to say that God will take him away by another force of nature. Like by your angry and spiteful community that will have lost their children and will want to kill your child. All I am doing here is creating a cause and effect situation in our timeline. That's why we never work against the will of God. I can't just go around helping people without realising the consequences it can bring. Do you understand what I am trying to say my good friend.

Mathew 24:7. [7] For nation shall rise against nation, and kingdom against kingdom: and there shall be famines, and pestilences, and earthquakes, in divers places.

Why do you think Greece is getting all of these earthquakes.

Because the prophecies of revalations are already well on the way. In fact we are smack bang in the middle of revalations as far as the bibles timeline is concerned. There are seven seals. The earth

Has already btokken 5 of them. The sixth seal will break when the rapture occurs. And the seventh seal represents seven trumpets. And they will blow during the great tribulation. And that is the second half of the antichrists reign. (the worst time in human history ever known to man). Everything that is written will come to pass

That is why not even all the earth angels in the world can save these children. It is written in the prophecies and it is God's will. South Africa have to pay for their sins. It's as simple as that. I know better than to fight the forces of God. So if I save your child don't come crying to me if he is murdered my friend. Us earth angels know how to look ahead about 6 moves. That is why we are all unbeatable at chess. And that was the hardest text I have ever had to write in my life. I can't write now because I am in tears.

I have just come into some knowledge about the antichrist.

The date is Feb 26 2025.

The antichrist is actually a spiritual being of pure white light glowing and emanating from all around him.

THAT IS HIS DECEPTION. He will pretend to be Jesus and the world will fall for it hook, line and sinker. For those who do no make the rapture all I can say is "Beware the DECEIVERS in RED " when the great tribulation begins. No other events have happened during this month except for the photos that I sent you.

And the children I am paying the hospital bills for in Nigeria are coping. But there has been no improvement. So that just confirms my worst nightmare of this pestilence that is sweeping the nations of Nigeria and kenya and Ghana.

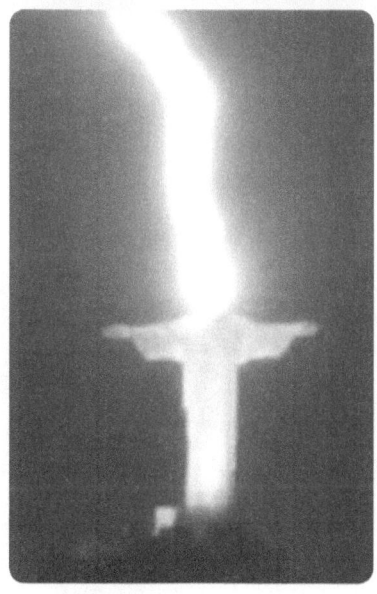